THE ILLUSTRATED

GEORGE HARRISON

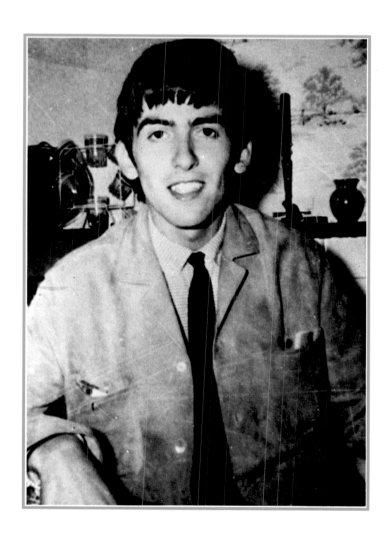

THE ILLUSTRATED
GEORGE HARRISON

GEOFFREY GIULIANO
BRENDA GIULIANO

SUNBURST BOOKS

DEDICATION

To His Divine Grace Om Visnupada Paramahamsa Parivrajakacarya Astottara-Sata Sri-Srimad B. H. Mangalniloy Goswami Maharaja our mentor and friend.

Published by Sunburst Books,
Deacon House, 65 Old Church Street, London SW3 5BS.

ISBN 1 85778 016 7

Printed and bound in Hong Kong

CONTENTS

CHAPTER ONE

EARTHBOUND

George Harold Harrison was born at 12.10 a.m., February 25, 1943. The philosophically minded Beatle later endeavoured to put a finger on the metaphysics involved in this, his latest incarnation:

To try and imagine the soul entering the womb of a woman living in 12 Arnold Grove, Wavertree, Liverpool 15. There were all the barrage balloons, and the Germans bombing Liverpool. All that was going on. I sat outside the house a couple of years ago, imagining 1943, nipping through the spiritual world, the astral level, getting back into a body in that house. That really is strange when you consider the whole planet, and all the planets there may be on the physical level. How do I come into that family, in that house at that time, and who am I anyway?

Mr. Harrison's first impression of his little son wasn't quite so lofty. "I vaguely remember tiptoeing up the stairs to see him after he was born," he said. "All I could think of was that he looked so remarkable like me! A tiny, squalling, miniature replica of myself."

At his mother's insistence, baby George was baptized a Catholic like the other children, although the Harrisons were admittedly not overtly religious.

George's mother recalls him as a toddler: "George was good as a child. He was no trouble at all and seldom misbehaved. Lots of people think maybe I say this because he's famous now, but he was good, so it would be unfair to say he was a naughty boy!"

George was very eager to start school. He was bright, intelligent and extremely independent. He was also very fair haired. He and his brother Pete were always together, and as a tot George would often look at photographs of his brother and think it was him. He never

Opposite: Arriving in India, 1966

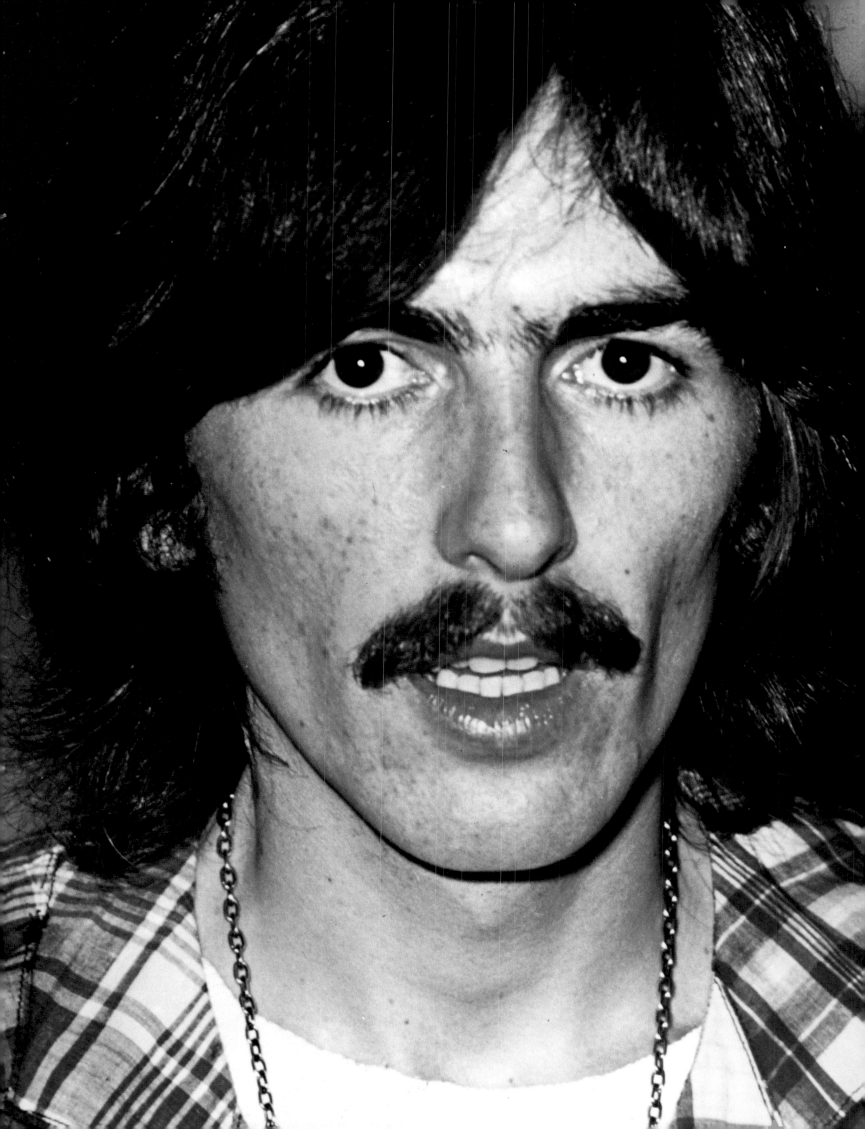

Schmoozing with Prime Minister, Harold Wilson, 1964

played about the streets as a child. He used to like swimming and always found something constructive to do in his spare time.

In 1949, the Harrisons moved from Wavertree to a brand-new, roomy council house in nearby Speke, which Harry had applied for some eighteen years earlier. The property, at 25 Upton Green, was lovely in comparison with Arnold Grove, but Louise didn't take to the sort of rough and tumble people who lived in the area and longed for the close familiarity of their old neighbourhood.

Harry Harrison remembers his wife taking eight-year-old George to the cinema and the boy insisting that she give an old tramp half a crown. "Money didn't mean anything to him even then," says Harry. "If George had his way, every old boy we saw should be entitled to at least a few pence. He was always very compassionate like that." Even today, Harrison hates to see street people hanging about in doorways or sleeping on the pavement. Once in the early eighties, as he was leaving a trendy London restaurant with friends "Legs" Larry Smith and Rolling Stone Bill Wyman, he offhandedly presented a destitute old man with a crisp fifty-pound note. According to Larry, it wasn't the first time he had seen the guitarist give so freely.

Although money in those days was usually quite tight, the Harrisons still tried to take a little family trip together at least once a year. Usually they went to nearby towns on the northwest coast - Bidston Hill, Southport, New Brighton and that standard British holiday resort, Blackpool. In his autobiography 'I Me Mine,' George recalls several childhood visits to Wales, where he marvelled at the country's natural beauty: "We went all over Wales, staying in little places, nice old stone cottages with slate roofs. Probably cost next to nothing to rent. You could actually live a whole happy life in a place like that."

On one holiday in Scotland, George was suddenly taken ill while swimming with his brothers at Inverness. A doctor was called and George was ordered into hospital. An ambulance arrived with two stretcher bearers, but George was adamant. "I'm not going on that," he said bluntly and walked out of the hotel, with the stretcher men in procession behind. In the hospital, George was far from a model patient. He hated the salt-free diet they put him on so much that he wrapped one meal in a brown paper bag and threw it out of a window when on one was looking. Unfortunately, the matron happened to be passing underneath at precisely that moment and caught the parcel right on her head. She strode purposefully up the stairs and into George's ward, only to find him apparently fast asleep. "He was the first person I have ever seen smiling that broadly in his sleep," she said dryly to his parents afterward.

Although George was certainly very intelligent and capable, he was never really fond of school. Bearing in mind George's outstanding creative achievements of later years, one might well assume that, in the eyes of his masters, anyway, the seemingly disinterested Harrison was a bit of an anomaly. "Little polite rows of toffee headed robots," John Lennon once said. "That's all any of [the teachers] were after."

The fabulous foursome assume a striking pose

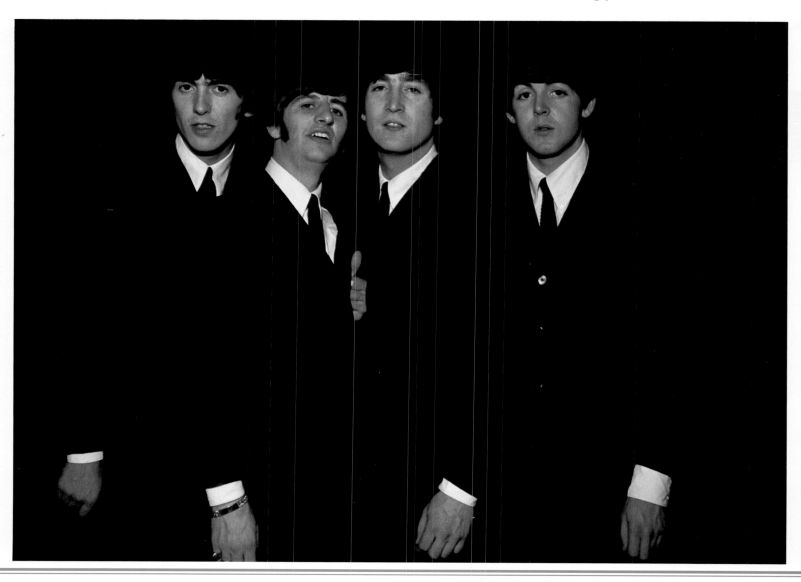

To George, seeing through the illusion of so-called adult authority seemed to be all the justification he needed to forever reject its dictates even at such an early age. Like so many others in the creative sphere, it was George himself who ultimately found the courage to reject the mores and values he saw around him. From "those nosey mothers" standing at the school gate to the unenlightened, interfering masters he met at school, George Harrison has never borne fools gladly.

After leaving Quarry Bank High School for Boys in 1953, George was enrolled at the Liverpool Institute. On his first day he was jumped from behind by a local roughneck, which did little to bolster his enthusiasm for his new school. At first, Harrison did try to make the best of things by attending classes and keeping up with his homework. But soon, as George put it, "the old rot set in," and he once again declared a war of in-attention on all things relating to his life at school.

A true rebel, by his sixteenth birthday George was at the very bottom of his class at the Liverpool Institute, and often in deep water at home. Although he made no bones about his feelings for school, he was secretly nervous about leaving without benefit of even the most basic qualifications. To be able to sit for the General Certificate of Education, a student had to first pass a preliminary exam given by his teachers. The minimum requirement was successful completion of at

Opposite: **Meeting the press at yet another fab Beatle press conference somewhere on the road, 1965**

Below: **Another silly photo opportunity with four very bored looking Beatles in Scotland, 1964**

Above: **Original Beatle drummer Pet Best in the garden of his mother's comfy suburban Liverpool home**

Below and opposite: **On the road with temporary Ringo replacement, Billy Nichols**

least three subjects relevant to one's choice of career. George, however, failed dismally in all his classes, except art. "While most of the other students spent their Wednesday afternoons panting around the school track," says George, "I was content to take a notebook and dream up some sketches. They were mostly from my head, not from anything around me. I was fond of sports, too, especially swimming, but I guess I was fonder of art."

Today, it is the little things George remembers about life in Liverpool, quirky, seemingly unrelated images strung together on a chain of golden memories. Pictures of pushy, tobacco-stained vicars chatting up housewives for donations. Little red-faced insurance salesmen toting their tatty imitation-leather briefcases around the noisy streets. Pot-bellied masters from the institute marching up and down the cricket fields followed by a scruffy band of schoolboy soldiers singing out their off-key cadence into Liverpool's late afternoon hustle-bustle. The rowdy merchant sailors, street vendors, pitiful alleyway drunkards, tight-lipped bobbies and, of course, the North's famous bounty of pretty girls. All characters right out of the Beatles' *Penny Lane*. All striking by their own peculiar sense of normalcy and all still very, very real to George Harrison.

There are magical places, too, that still simmer fondly in George's consciousness. A highly polished giant meteorite set into cement out-

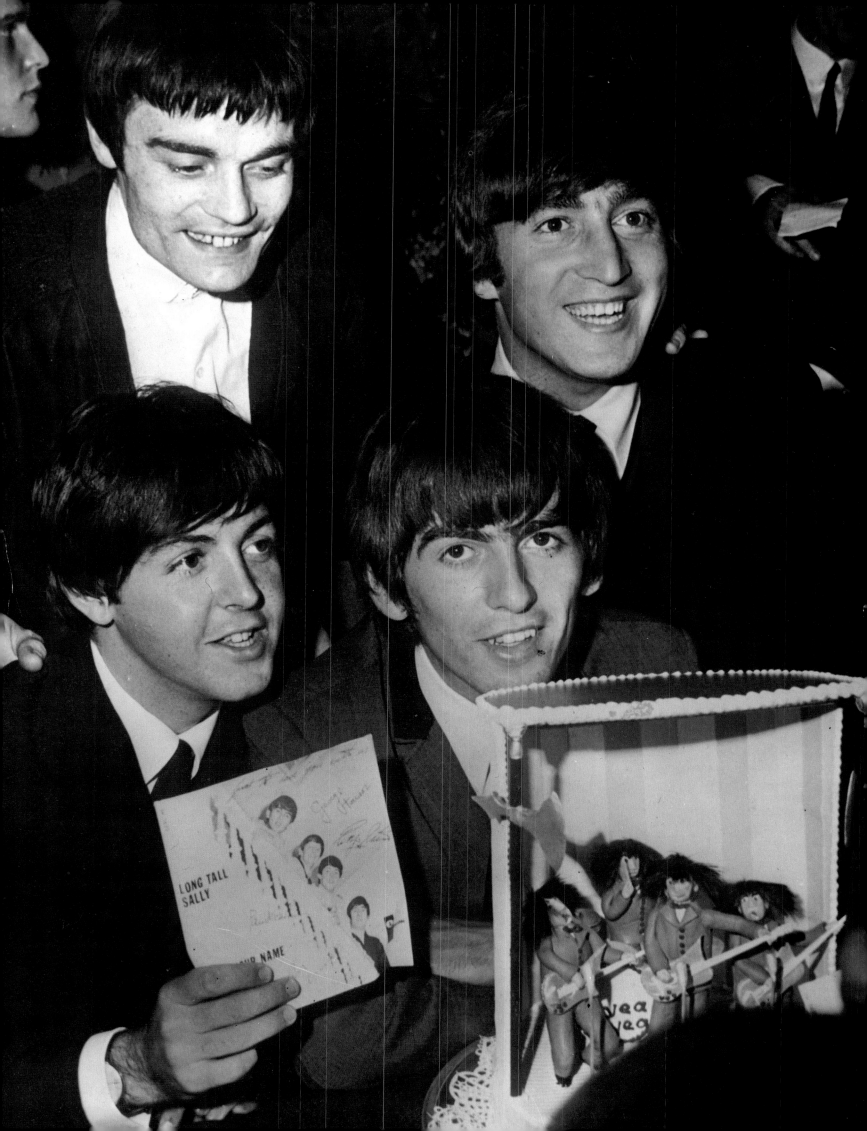

side the Wavertree Baths that, after careering around the Milky Way for a million years or so finished up its journey in a farmer's muddy field in suburban Liverpool. Young George used to scramble up on top and then gaily slide back down. It is still there today. Then there were Calderstone Park, the library and the mysterious tunnels leading the way to Childwall Five Ways. None of these places are on the tourist maps handed to out-of-town Beatle fans by the Merseyside Tourist Board. These are secret places reserved only for the people of Liverpool. The real Liverpool. The Liverpool Carl Jung called "the pool of life." The heady stuff that dreams are made of. And about which songs are composed and sung.

Above: **john and George asleep at the wheel riding on the Magical Mystery Tour**

Opposite: **George and Pattie, young and in love way back when**

CHAPTER TWO

RIDING THE WHEEL

Louise Harrison's first indication that George was seriously interested in music came when he was thirteen; she happened to notice that his school exercise books were virtually covered with crude little sketches of guitars. Soon afterward, she bought her son a cheap three-pound acoustic from the father of one of George's schoolmates. Surprisingly, George didn't seem interested and relegated the gift to an upstairs cupboard for the next three months. When he eventually picked it up he found it frustratingly difficult to learn and almost packed it in several times before finally making a little progress. Sitting up some nights till nearly dawn, with his mum to encourage him, he practiced until his fingers bled.

With practice and determination - often listening to pop records and then trying to mimic what he'd just heard - George began to play quite well and outgrew the battered old acoustic that had served him so faithfully. His mum once again came to the rescue by saving up her extra household money to buy him another guitar. This one, a good, solid, wide-body acoustic with white inlaid trim, cost thirty pounds and featured a handy cutaway neck for easier maneuverability on the lower frets of the fingerboard. Proud and independent, young George was determined to reimburse his mother as soon as he could. It just wasn't in the lad's makeup to accept from anyone what he considered charity. As a result, he soon signed on as a Saturday-afternoon delivery boy for a local butcher. George's natural aversion to flesh as food slowly gained momentum as he cycled through the narrow back streets of Speke with a full load of raw meat packed into his dusty saddle bags. It is tempting to speculate whether these early memories later inspired his militant anti-meat eating song *Piggies* on the Beatles'

White album.

Still marking time at the Liverpool Institute, George shuttled back and forth to school on his father's bus from Speke to Liverpool in a dreamy haze of guitars and pop stars. The long, rambling ride took up to an hour each way, which also allowed him the boyhood luxury of mucking about with the other lads. One of the boys, the son of a cotton salesman and the estate midwife from Allerton, was especially good fun. His name was Paul McCartney, and although he was a year ahead of George at school, the two quickly became firm friends by early 1955. Like George, McCartney was also intensely interested in music and not only played the guitar but also held the proud distinction of owning his very own trumpet, which greatly impressed young master Harrison.

At home, George used to perch himself on a stool in the middle of the sitting room and strum along to his favourite skiffle tunes with his brother Pete, a fair musician himself. The two brothers even played a

George and John in a humourous skit included in the 1964 film *Around the Beatles*

Overleaf: At Brian Epstein's posh Belgravia home, 1967

17

Arriving at Apple, 1968

With John, being interviewed by David Frost

gig together at the British Legion Club in Speke in 1956 with Pete's school chum Arthur Kelly, and one or two others calling themselves the Rebels. This first engagement was memorable in that none of the other groups scheduled to play turned up, so the rocking Rebels were forced to entertain for the entire evening.

Paul McCartney first laid eyes on John Lennon at, of all places, the neighbourhood chip shop. McCartney was invited to join the Quarry Men on the merit of his mastery of *Twenty Flight Rock*, as well as his justly famous Little Richard imitation. His obvious talents were a welcome addtion to the rag-tag group of schoolboy musicians. "John was really the only oustanding member," says Paul. "All the rest sort of slipped way, you know? I suppose the drummer was pretty good actually, for what we knew then. Frankly, one of the reasons they all liked Colin (Hanton) was because he happened to have the (Coasters') record *Searchin*, and that was pretty impressive currency back then. I mean, sometimes you made a whole career with someone solely on the basis of them owning a particular record!"

Deeply drawn in by the charismatic spell cast by the masterful Lennon, young Paul McCartney reveled in his role as John's onstage foil and steady street-corner accomplice. But though their musical efforts within the admittedly shaky structure of the Quarry Men were both admirable and ambitious, what they really needed was a good, solid lead guitar upon which to hang their funky back-street skiffle sound. Paul remembers the events leading up to their settling on George: "Well, he was always my little mate. Nonetheless, he could really play guitar, particularly this piece called *Raunchy*, which we all

used to love. You see, if anyone could do something like that it was generally enough to get them in the group. Of course, I knew George long before any of the others, as they were all from Woolton and we hung out with the Allerton set. I can tell you we both learned guitar from the same book, and that despite his tender years, we were chums."

John Lennon, however, was apparently quite skeptical about admitting such a veritable baby into the group. How would it look for someone as talented and popular as John to be caught consorting with someone so young and obviously undistinguished as George? What would his mates think, let alone the ladies? After all, the whole point of being in a band in the first place was to look like a big man, and that was admittedly a little tough to do playing with a teenybopper guitarist like George. In the end, however, Harrison's exceptional musical skill coupled with McCartney's insistence that George be brought on board overruled John's initial reservations.

George played *Raunchy* for them in a cellar club called the Morgue, then hung around the band until he was invited to play with them. He was formally accepted as a member on February 6, 1958.

McCartney, however, tells a slightly different tale. He says George's audition took place atop a Liverpool-bound bus: "George slipped quietly into one of the seats aboard this largely deserted bus we were riding, took out his guitar and went right into *Raunchy*. A few days later I

The Beatles as we remember them best

Opposite: **Sweating out the licks on stage, 1964**

said to John, "Well, what do you think?" And he finally says, "Yeah, man, he'd be great!". And that was simply that. George was in."

One of the boys' first big breaks came when Britain's "Mr. Star Maker," Caroll Levis, announced to the papers in November 1959 that he would soon be holding auditions at the empire Theatre in Liverpool for his Caroll Levis "Discoveries" television program, which was to be filmed at a Manchester studio some weeks later. As expected, virtually every guitar-toting teenager in town turned out for the big event including, of course, John, Paul and George, this time billing themselves as the Moondogs. Louise Harrison remembers George being

absolutely "over the moon" when he received word of their selection:

They let us know by post. At first I couldn't make out why anyone would send us a letter addressed to the "Moondogs," but then I twigged. "You must have won, son!" I shouted to George, who happened to be just at the top of the stairs getting ready to go out. "I can't believe it!" he cried, almost flying down the stairs to read the letter. "We're really on the way now!"

The evening of the big show, the boys boarded the train from Liverpool's Lime Street Station to Manchester, struggling down the platform with their guitars and primitive amplifiers tottering precariously atop a luggage cart. "Where are we going, fellas?" Lennon sang out as they made their way into the already rolling train. "To the top, Johnny!" they yelled. "Where's that, lads?" "Why, to the toppermost of the poppermost!"

Although the Moondogs gave a rousing performance that night, they were in jeopardy of missing the last train back to Liverpool and couldn't therefore, stay for the final judging. It was a crushing disappointment to the starry-eyed young musicians, being so close to what they considered "the big time," only to have it elude them through something so simple as the lack of reliable transport. For this night, anyway, "the toppermost of the poppermost" would remain just a distant dream.

Top: **The Beatles live, 1964**

Above: **Bryan Epstein's stylish Liverpool grave**

Opposite: **Touching down in San Francisco to perform their last ever scheduled concert**

CHAPTER THREE

INSIDE OUT

"There was a time when George really had no faith at all that the Beatles would ever click," Harry Harrison senior has said. "I remember him going on about the lot of us packing up and emigrating to Australia. Then it was Canada, and even Malta for a time. "Just stick with the music, boy," I told him. "If you really want it bad enough you'll catch your star."

Of all the Beatles, George Harrison was perhaps the least likely to have stayed in show business if the Beatles hadn't finally caught on. Adventure was what he was after, and money. In their early days with manager Brian Epstein, it was Harrison who was most concerned with the business of contracts and record royalties. In the early days of rock and roll, playing music had not so much to do with artistry as with setting one's self above the crowd. Says Harrison wryly: "We looked at fellas like Buddy Holly and Elvis and thought, "That looks like a good job." Money, travel, chicks, nice threads - there's a great deal to be said for playing rock and roll."

The boys' first notable tour was in May 1960, when they backed pop singer Johnny Gentle in Scotland on what Harrison's buddy "Legs" Larry Smith has called "the cellotape and chewing gum circuit." The two-week tour took the band - now called the Silver Beatles - to the northernmost tip of Scotland, where they played dingy working-men's clubs and tatty teenage ballrooms all along the eastern coast. John's art-school chum, bass player Stuart Sutcliffe, by now had joined the band, as had drummer Tommy Moore. To affect a more "professional" air, the young men adopted stage names. George became Carl Harrison, after his rock idol, Carl Perkins; John was renamed Johnny Silver; Paul was now Paul Raymon; Stu became Stu de Stael. Tommy

Opposite: Cutting the cake

George and Pattie on their wedding day

Below: **Batchelor Harrison signing his life away**

Moore did not change his name.

By early summer of 1960, the prospects for the band were dwindling. By all accounts Tommy Moore had been quite good on the skins, but, being significantly older than the others, wasn't about to make a career of bashing about with a local two-bit beat group. A month after the tour (during which Tommy had the misfortune of losing his two front teeth when the group's van collided with a car full of senior citizens), Moore unceremoniously bailed out.

The effect on the band was devastating, for no one would ever hire them without a drummer. Fortunately, the answer to the Beatles' prayers soon came in the person of Randolph Peter Best, a strikingly handsome though sometimes uncomfortably quiet young man. Not only did he have a gear new kit but his mum, Mona, also had her own teen club, an irresistible combination.

Touring San Franciso's hippie haven, Haight-Ashbury, 1968

A few months later, Allan Williams, the diabolical Welshman who had arranged some earlier bookings for the boys, was in a trendy London coffee bar called the Two I's, when he ran into German night-club owner Bruno Koschmider. "Do you think you could fix me up with a Liverpool group to take back home?" Kischmider enquired. "Sure thing," Williams shot back. "One of the city's best."

The band he had in mind was Derry and the Seniors, a well-organised beat group much loved in Merseyside. Their gig went well, and soon Williams was again called upon to help import more of Liverpool's raucous brand of rock and roll to Hamburg's music-loving teens. This time, though, the boys were not passed over. Despite strong objections from their families, in August 1960 the Beatles piled into Williams's battered van and barrelled off to the Channel ferry and on to Germany.

George Harrison once listed his tour of duty in Hamburg as his only "higher education," and he wasn't far wrong. To the Beatles, Hamburg's raw, uncensored lifestyle gave them a kind of carte blanche to act out their most violent and aggressive fantasies.

Altogether, the Beatles' first trek to Hamburg lasted just over four months. Although they found playing the Kaiserkeller infinitely prefer-

able to the cramped and seedy Indra, they weren't entirely happy with Bruno Koschmider's bullying tactics, nor with the deplorable living conditions they were forced to endure. As a result, they approached local club manager Peter Eckhorn and requested an audition with an eye toward transferring their talents to his Top Ten Club, an even grander version of the somewhat scruffy Kaiserkeller.

The Top Ten was anxious to have the Beatles as their star attraction, but Bruno Koschmider was very distressed at the thought of losing his biggest draw to the competition. Unfortunately for Koschmider, the Beatles' contract with him was about to expire, leaving the group free to perform wherever they chose. And they wasted no time. One evening, without any notice, the boys were gone, off to play the Top Ten for their new boss, Peter Eckhorn. As far as the Beatles were concerned, after having lived rough for so long, their only loyalty now was to themselves.

They were quite pleased with their new position. Their accommodations, supplied courtesy of Eckhorn, were far more comfortable than the smelly lodgings they shared at the Bambi Kino, and the pay was top-notch. With a new extended contract in hand, it looked as though things were finally beginning to go their way.

Precisely twenty-four hours after the boys moved into their new rooms, they were awakened by a loud knock at the door. "Police! You must open up!" The boys scrambled out of bed and hurried to get dressed. Lennon stumbled into the hallway and cracked open the door just enough to make sure their visitors weren't a team of Koschmider's musclebound enforcers sent round to make the lads an offer they couldn't refuse. That was the only invitation the police required, though, and suddenly the room was wall to wall uniforms. "We are looking for the one called Harrison," one of the cops barked. Everyone froze. "What the fuck do you want him for?" said Lennon, surprisingly belligerent in the face of such authority. "He hasn't done anything."

Apparently the police had received an anonymous tip that George was only seventeen and was therefore too young to be playing in an adult club past curfew. On top of that, the Beatles had not bothered to secure either visas or work permits before the band came to perform in Germany. George was to be deported immediately. There was no way out of this one; the boys had been had, by someone with a grudge. Someone very like Bruno Kischmider.

The loss of their guitar player left the Beatles in an awkward position. They couldn't very well perform without him, and there was little hope that the German authorities would relent and allow them to stay. They had no choice but to make their way home as best they could.

By early spring of 1961, the Beatles were one of Merseyside's top bands but were still virtually unknown outside their hometown. By now George had turned eighteen, so the group returned to Hamburg to play the Top Ten, from April through July 1961. While there, they

Opposite: Sharing a joke during the filming of *A Hard Day's Night*

had been invited to sit in on a recording session with transplanted English pop singer Tony Sheridan, who was perhaps Hamburg's most popular entertainer. Although the Beatles had recorded a few times previously, once as the Quarry Men in a friend's basement studio in Liverpool and then in the fall of 1960 at Akustik Studios in Hamburg, these were their first truly professional sessions. Produced by the well-known orchestra leader Bert Kaempfert, the boys recorded eight tunes: six backing Sheridan, and two others, a rocked-up version of *My Bonnie* and a Harrison-Lennon original, *Cry for a Shadow*. Released as a single in Germany in August 1961, a few imported copies of *My Bonnie* made their way back to England and before long the obscure 45 was occasionally being spun in a few Liverpool-area discos. All of which prompted eighteen-year-old Raymond Jones to wander into local businessman Brian Epstein's NEMS (North East Music Stores) shop in the Whitechapel section of Liverpool on October 28, 1961, and request a copy of the hard-to-find single.

Epstein had always prided himself on his ability to rustle up even the most obscure records for his customers, but this particular order had

Yet another happy airport reception, 1965

him stumped. What's more, none of Brian's many contacts in the music business had even heard of the band, much less their fly-by-night single. Coincidentally, a couple of weeks later, while chatting with one of his sales-clerks, he learned that the mystery group was playing only a few hundred feet away at the tiny basement club on Matthew Street. He was intrigued.

A little after noon on November 9, 1961, Brian and his personal assistant, Alistair Taylor, visited the Cavern to hear for themselves this swinging ensemble known as the Beatles. Thirty-four days later, during a meeting at Pete Best's house, a formal management agreement was negotiated between the Beatles and Epstein's NEMS Enterprises. Brian didn't actually sign the document but simply shook hands as a show of faith. After all, unlike these four young scruffs, Epstein was a gentleman and his word was therefore his bond. At any rate, the deal was done. The Beatles finally had themselves an official manager and Epstein yet another pet project to occupy his otherwise tediously lonely life. Little did either party suspect what was to happen to them all in just a few short months.

Posing with Billy Nichols

Harrison and a host of superstar friends join John and Yoko's *War Is Over* poster campaign

Opposite and overleaf: **At the world's first live international satellite broadcast *Our World*, at EMI Studios, Abbey Road,**

By the fall of 1963, full-tilt, gut-wrenching, diehard Beatlemania had descended upon the British Isles. By Christmastime the band had played the prestigious Royal Variety Performance, toured Sweden, scored a number-one single with *" Want to Hold Your Hand* and consummated the deal for their first full-length motion picture, *A Hard Day's Night.*

In January 1964 *I Want to Hold Your Hand* entered the American record charts at number 83. By the next week it had climbed steadily to 42 and showed no signs of levelling off. Days later, while the Beatles were holed up in their ritzy digs at the famous Hotel George V near the Champs-Elysees in Paris, they received a call from New York informing them that their turbulent teenage love call had toppled Bobby Vinton's *"There! I've Said It Again* and was now number one on the charts. Everyone was ecstatic. It was a dream come true. The boys had already experienced the thrill of topping the charts back home. Now they were taking America!

On board Pan Am flight 101 from London's Heathrow to New York's Kennedy Airport, on February 7, 1964, George Harrison and his three colleagues were very anxious. "America's got everything," thought Harrison out loud. "Why should they want us?" On top of feeling almost unbearable apprehension, George was also sick with the flu and concerned that his hair didn't look quite right following a last-minute shampoo back in London (no small worry to a group for whom hair was such an important part of the act).

Brian Epstein, meanwhile, though trying to appear calm, was concerned that Harrison's ill health would prevent him from playing either "The Ed Sullivan Show" or Carnegie Hall.

From the moment they landed on American soil, everything went at breakneck speed. As the plane slowly made its way to the gate, the shrill screams of more than ten thousand hysterical teenagers pene-

trated the hull of the aircraft. Peering through the windows of the DC 10, the boys thought that perhaps the president was about to land on another runway.

"Every kid from Broadway to the Bronx is here," observed one seasoned veteran of the New York press corps in an on-the-spot report. "They're wearing buttons that say 'I Like the Beatles,' and waving home-made banners. Teenaged girls are fainting by the dozen, and we've even seen a few of the older cops sticking bullets in their ears, for Pete's sake. As far as I can tell the four Beatles are standing at the door of the aircraft almost certainly completely and utterly in shock. No one, I mean no one, has ever seen or even remotely suspected anything like this before!"

After their first appearance on "The Ed Sullivan Show," which was seen by a record 73 million viewers, the entourage boarded a train

George's boyhood home in Liverpool and the young lad who lives there now

Brian Epstein's posh NEMs business office, circa 1965

bound for Washington D.C., on the morning of February 11. That night they played before twenty-thousand screaming fans at the Coliseum, another record audience and the first of many manic concerts the Fab Four were forced to endure. "It was bloody awful," says Harrison.

From February 2, 1963, to August 29, 1966, the Beatles played more than 225 live shows in almost every country of the free world. They performed for millions of hysterical teenyboppers, were pelted with jelly beans and constantly harassed by fans looking for souvenirs - everything from autographs to bits of their hair, clothes and even fingernails. Crippled children were wheeled into the boys' dressing rooms in hopes that a dose of their mysterious power might restore or straighten lifeless limbs and twisted bodies. Airport terminals were continually dirtied by young women who became incontinent when at last they caught up with their favourite Beatle. It was, in all, quite a lot of madness for four provincial young men from the north of England to endure. And so, when the Beatles laid down their instruments after their last number at Candlestick Park in San Francisco on August 29, 1966, they said goodbye to public performing forever.

From then on, John, Paul, George and Ringo would devot themselves exclusively to working their magic only in the privacy and sanctity of the recording studio. George Harrison, for one, couldn't have been more pleased.

CHAPTER FOUR

BAD WORDS

Back in the late sixties while many of the world's youth were busy getting loaded with their friends and living off student loans, George Harrison had already taken on a world of responsibility. He became one-fourth of the Beatles' international Apple Corps Limited, as well as being a fulltime professional musician, composer, record producer and husband. During this period, Harrison was now determined to forge a more meaningful role for himself within the group. Notwithstanding the Beatles' musical Midas touch, George became keen to launch his own solo career as well.

"I got back from (the Maharishi's retreat in) India a bit later than everybody else," George recalled in the mid-seventies. "They all split and started Apple. When I got back it was like a madhouse. In fact, to this day we're still trying to untangle it. At that time John and Yoko had just gotten together, and they had some guy throwing the I Ching every ten minutes. 'Oh we're having a business meeting? Then let's play the I Ching!' The place was full of lunatics."

Apple Corps Limited was established late in 1967 chiefly as a device for lessening the Beatles' incredible tax burden. Paul McCartney came up with the name after apparently being inspired by an original Magritte painting he owned, which featured a giant Granny Smith apple locked inside a tidy room.

The first Beatle-related venture to carry the Apple logo was the film *Magical Mystery Tour*, shown on English television on December 26, 1967. Artistically, it was years ahead of its time, employing many of the same surreal techniques so popular in today's rock videos. Commercially, however it was a disaster.

From there Apple evolved into a trendy high-fashion head shop and

boutique housed at 94 Baker Street, in Sherlock Holmes territory, with a small music publishing division housed above the store. In those days, Mike Berry, a middle-management music executive, and Beatle buddy Terry Doran were running the show, assisted by two attractive but largely ineffectual secretaries.

The Apple Boutique opened its doors on December 7, 1967, with a gala celebration attended by John, George, their wives and about two hundred more trendy people than could comfortably fit inside the store. John nicknamed it the "psychaedelic Woolworth's", and almost immediately it became the place to see and be seen in Swinging London. The shopfront featured a far-out, acid-inspired mural by a team of Dutch designers who called themselves The Fool. After endearing themselves to the Beatles, the flamboyant artists proceeded to put their creative touch to just about everything the boys owned. Suddenly, wild rainbow-coloured designs showed up on George's living-room fireplace and on one or two of his favourite guitars. John even commissioned a fancy paint job for an antique upright piano.

Harrison's photographic self portrait with celebrated sitarist Shambu Das on Juhu Beach, Bombay, 1966

However impressed the Beatles may have been with The Fool's far-out creations, their Baker Street neighbours were less favourably disposed and promptly petitioned city officials to have the offending dreamscape removed from the building. About eight months later, the shop was closed down after a long history of petty pilfering and poor management, and the entire contents given away free to the public - that is, after the boys stopped by to do a little last-minute shopping themselves.

Still cautiously optimistic about their future together, from 1966 to 1969 the Beatles racked up an incredible list of worldwide smash recordings, the titles of which read like a table of contents for the dope-filled dreams of an entire generation: *Rubber Soul*, *Revolver*, *Sgt. Pepper's Lonely Hearts Club Band*, *Magical Myster Tour*, *The Beatles* (the *White* album), the *Yellow Submarine* soundtrack, *Abbey Road* and *Let It Be* - an astounding array of ground-breaking, intelligent and artfully conceived music. The problem was that the evolving talents of the four artists could no longer be so easily contained on one LP every twelve months or so. There is no doubt that George Harrison pos-

Below: An impromptu sitar lesson in the Beatles' hotel suite, 1966

Opposite: **With the Maharishi in London, 1967**

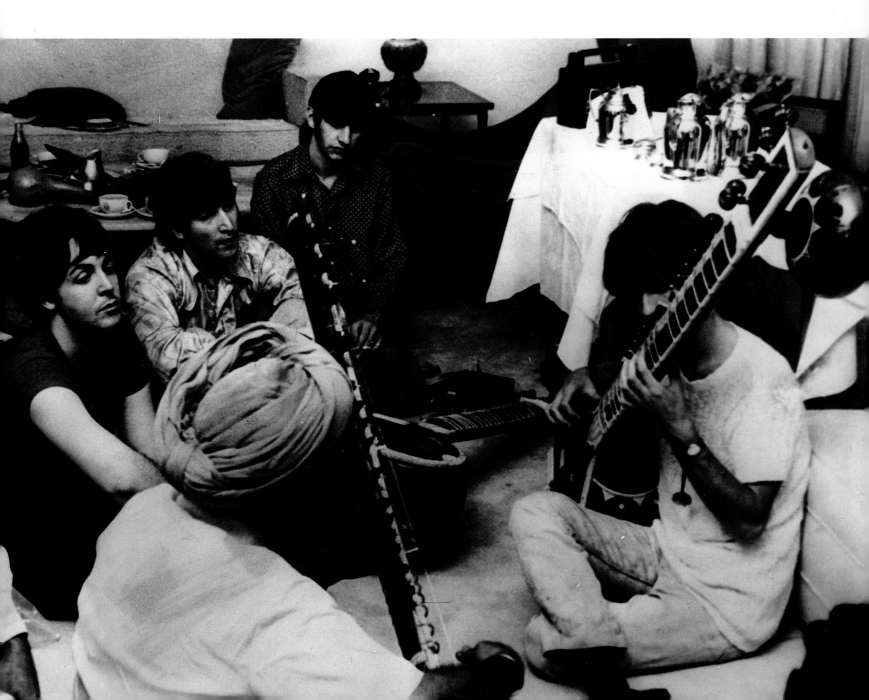

Right: **On stage, 1974**

Opposite: **At the press launch for Harrison's pet project, The Radha Krishna Temple's Apple LP of the same name**

Previous page: **Posing at the guru's swank Himalayan ashram in Rishikesh**

sessed the innate ability to perhaps even commercially surpass the Lennon-McCartney songwriting cartel, but the chance never came, and Harrison was relegated by fate to the back of the Beatles' bus to ride out the remainder of the Mystery Tour as a second-class citizen. "I believe that if I'm going to sing songs on record, they might as well be my own," commented George in 1969.

I also feel you can say more in two minutes of a song than in ten years. The first song I ever wrote was *Don't Bother Me*. It wasn't very good, but I was sick in bed and I thought I might as well write something, and it went on our second album (*With the Beatles*; released in America as *Meet the Beatles*). The most difficult thing for me is following Paul's and John's songs. Their earlier songs weren't as good as they are now, though, and they obviously got better and better, and that's what I have to do. I've got about forty tunes that I haven't recorded, and some of them are quite good. I wrote one called *The Art*

of Dying (later to appear on *All Things Must Pass*) three years ago, and at the time I thought it was too far out. But I'm still going to record it.

I used to have a hang-up about telling John, Paul and Ringo I had a song for the albums, because I felt mentally, at that time, as if I was trying to compete. And in a way, the standard of the songs had to be good, because theirs were very good. I don't want the Beatles to be recording rubbish for my sake ... just because I wrote it. On the other hand, I don't want to record rubbish, just because they wrote it. The group comes first. It took time for me to get more confidence as a songwriter, and now I don't care if they don't like it. I can shrug it off. Sometimes it's a matter of whoever pushes hardest gets the most tunes on the album, then it's down to personalities. And more often, I just leave it until somebody would like to do one of my tunes.

The late sixties seemed to be rather an era of disillusionment for George Harrison. First it was the broken promise of drug-induced enlightenment, followed closely by the inevitable wilting of flower power. The Beatles' trek to India in 1967 to sit at the feet of the Maharishi turned sour almost immediately, and even George's fairy-tale marriage to Pattie Boyd began to suffer under the strain of the constant demands made upon George's time and energy. When the Beatles finally began to collapse in 1969, Harrison's new declaration of

Below and opposite top: **Recording the popular Zapple release** *Wonderwall* **in India, 1967**

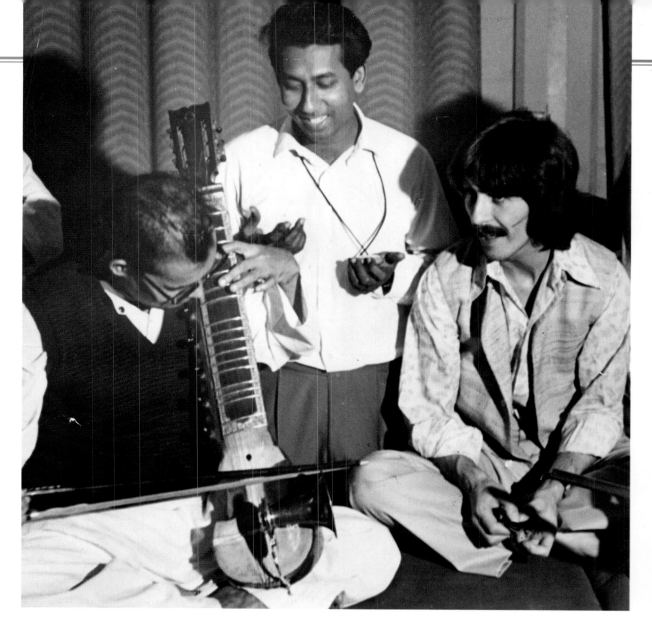

George
demonstrates his
sitar technique to
British film star Rita
Tushingham, 1966

George

Previous page: **Happy and high in the court of Sexy Sadie,1967**

Below: **With the Maharishi before the Beatles final disillusionment, 1967**

Opposite: **Harrison at the heady height of his lifelong Hindu obsession**

independence was tempered, it was safe to say, with some very real doubts.

Like the sweet twirling smoke of an Indian joss stick, the swinging sixties faded into the uncertain seventies and scattered to ashes any hopes the world might have had that the Beatles would stay together. When at last it came, on December 31, 1970, with the suit McCartney brought against his three former partners, the end was long overdue. In even the most bitter of marriages, the mechanics of the final dissolution are always painful. Anger is the first emotion to be overcome, and in the case of John, Paul, George and Ringo, that alone took years.

People, of course, are desperate to try to pinpoint a specific cause of the split - something absolute to tidy up all the loose ends in their minds. The truth is it was many things, but mostly just the inevitable ebb and flow of time washing away what was and replacing it with what is.

One of the most profound reasons, however, seems to be the introduction of New York show business accountant Allen Klein into the picture back in 1969. Eventually, John, George, and Ringo were convinced that Klein just might be the answer to the Beatles' problems with Apple and as a group. Paul McCartney, however, and apparently quite a few

other Apple insiders, definitely did not agree.

Being in the Beatles, in Harrison's words, was like "being in a box," and once the way was finally made clear, he ran like blazes and never looked back. Although they are all genuinely loving, none of the Beatles is particularly sentimental or nostalgic. On the surface, at least, there is a hardness that probably owes much to being from the north of England, but even more to having lived through the lunacy of Beatlemania. When they went their separate ways, George was only too pleased to try to deflate the group's mighty myth at every turn.

"I realise that we did fill a big gap in the sixties," he has said, "but all the people who we really meant something to are all grown up. It's like anything people gorw up with, they get attached to it. I can understand that the Beatles, in many ways, did some nice things, and it's very appreci-

The Maharishi Mahesh Yogi at Euston Station, London, 1967

ated that people still like them. But the problem comes when they want to live in the past."

As a roving one-man anti-Beatles propaganda machine, George had a mighty tough row to hoe. Still, he makes a lot of sense. "Even if I were to be a Beatle for the rest of my life, it would still be only a temporary thing," he says, referring to the transitory nature of life itself.

As the years slipped away, however, Harrison's hard-line view on the Fab Four loosened up considerably: "Maybe one day we'll get the Beatles together and just put them in a room having tea, satellite it all over the world and charge twenty dollars each to watch it. We could make a fortune."

By the mid-seventies Harrison was able to see the whole amazing period with at least a measure of good humour.

Opposite: George Harrison circa 1969

GOD'S EYE

From the first eerie twang of the Indian sitar in the motion-picture soundtrack of the Beatles' second feature film, Help!, George Harrison was forever hooked. From that moment on, all things Hindu - philosophy, diet, fashion, literature and art - held their transcendent sway over the young man, who shuttled his revelations across the Indian subcontinent into the appreciative arms of a turned-on generation of seekers. Suddenly, in tiny bedrooms and cluttered crash pads around the world, young people were ripping down their tattered M.C. Escher posters in favour of brightly coloured representations of an array of multiarmed benevolent gods from Buddha to Brahma. At the very hub of this spiritual revolution was George's friend and mentor, sitar virtuoso Ravi Shankar.

"I met him at Peter Sellers' house in London for dinner," recalled George of their introduction in 1966, "and he offered to give me some instruction on the basics of sitar. It was the first time I'd ever actually approached music with a bit of discipline. Later, I started really listening to Indian music, and for the next two years I hardly even touched the guitar, except for recording. Having all these material things ... I still wanted something more, and it suddenly came to me in the form of Ravi Shankar."

By the late summer of 1967, both George and Pattie Harrison had become absorbed in cultivating their spiritual lives. They had already endeavoured to teach themselves meditation from books but weren't really making much headway. So when a girlfriend of Pattie's suggested that she attend a lecture on Transcendental Meditation at Caxton Hall, London, she readily accepted and afterward signed up to become a member.

Opposite: **The Harrisons leave Esher Town Court following a brief trial that ultimately led to the couple being convicted of possessing hashish. Although they only recieved a small fine, the drug conviction caused George, in particular, significant imigration hassles.**

George, meanwhile, alerted the other Beatles that the Maharishi Mahesh Yogi was coming to London and they could hear him speak at the Hilton Hotel on August 24. They went, and were impressed by what they heard. Afterward, the Maharishi met the boys and invited them to a ten-day conference in Bangor, North Wales, the next day. Travelling with the guru by train (or "The Mystical Special" as the London Daily Mirror called it) were Mick Jagger, Marianne Faithfull, and Pattie's younger sister, Jenny Boyd, among others. George especially was genuinely excited about the prospect of finally hooking up with someone who, it seemed, might be able to provide some answers to the Beatles' nonstop, topsy-turvy existence. Naturally, the platform at Bangor was mobbed by hundreds of screaming fans. John Lennon later confided that the naive yogi actually thought the crowds turned out to see him.

On August 27, 1967, the Beatles were formally initiated into his society some distressing news suddenly came through from London - Brian Epstein was dead.

Although the Beatles were naturally concerned about how Epstein's untimely demise might affect their careers, and thus their staggering

Opposite: **Singing Hare Krishna, 1969.**

Below: **Perhaps the two most famous faces of the Swinging Sixties**

Relaxing at home in Henley, 1970

collective fortunes, for George Harrison the tragedy only encouraged his further retreat into the yogic philosophy that by now consumed him.

Still, it was with great enthusiasm and optimism all round that George, John, their wives and a few close friends arrived at New Delhi Airport on the morning of February 16, 1968, to begin serious study with the Maharishi at his extravagant Rishikesh retreat.

As one day slipped casually into the next and the initial excitement of the trip subsided, the boys' pent-up tensions slowly began to unravel under the magic spell of the meditation. Most days it was the normally sluggish John who was the first up, and after about a half-hour of meditation he would go for a leisurely stroll round the compound with Mal or George.

Soon, however, the inevitable happened, and the Beatles' fascination with TM slowly began to subside. After all, sitting hour after hour silently muttering a Sanskrit syllable to oneself (no matter how exotic the locale) did tend to become a little boring. Ringo and his wife, Maureen, left after only ten days.

McCartney, meanwhile, was becoming increasingly anxious over the preliminary organisation of Apple, a pet project meant to bring at least a semblance of order to the Beatles' rapidly declining business empire. Despite the distractions, however, Paul and his girlfriend, actresss Jane Asher, managed to stick it out for six weeks before jetting off home. Were they disillusioned with the teaching? They were asked upon their return. "No," said Paul, "just a little homesick."

That left John and George, the Maharishi's most ardent believers. So besotted were they with the bearded holy man that even when "Magic" Alex first introduced a rumour that the Maharishi had made a very definite bid for the earthly affections of Mia Farrow, they were loath to believe it. Within a week Farrow had gone on a tiger hunt in the south. It was suggested by the Maharishi's staff that she would be returning shortly thereafter. She never did.

John and George were extremely hurt and confused by the whole sordid affair, all the while enthusiastically counselled by their mate "Magic" Alex to drop the guru once and for all and go home.

The Beatles stormed out of the bungalow and rang for a taxi from the ashram's dining hall before racing back to their quarters to pack. As they were filing out the main gate, a disciple was sent by the Maharishi to make one last pitiful plea for them to calm down and talk things over. But it was too late. The Beatles, like so many times in the past, had burned their bridges and were moving on.

Arriving for sessions for the Beatles' *Abbey Road*

There isn't much doubt that the Harrisons' admittedly jet-set lifestyle was both a blessing and a curse to their yoga practice. On one hand, their social mobility gave them access to virtually anyone they wanted to meet; on the other, it threw a lot of fuel on the fire of passions they were both struggling to control. For George and Pattie Harrison their abiding interest in Krishna consciousness was a double-edged sword. The transcendental power of the mantra was both liberating and inspirational, but the rigid dictates of their "new" guru Srila Prabhupada's no-nonsense philosophy tended to expose faint cracks in their already shaky marriage.

By early 1973 George was more involed than ever with the London Radha Krishna Temple. When Prabhupada noted that because of growing attendance their London property was no longer suitable, Harrison readily agreed to finance the acquisition of yet another house. This time it should be something really grand, some place with prestige to help attract a more select following, and preferably in the country with large grounds to accommodate the many outdoor festivals held each year. In short, a real showplace for Krishna consciousness. A place where people could get a taste of the splendor of devotional service to the Supreme Lord. A tall order, to be sure, but after all, it wasn't every day a Beatle got to go house-hunting for God!

Eventually they found the perfect site in what was to become Bhaktivedanta Manor, in Letchmoore Heath, just outside London. George negotiated down the exorbitant asking price, then bought the

Exiting Abbey Road

Opposite: **John and Yoko, 1969, a time when none of the Beatles really had much to say to each other**

property. In early March 1973, the Krishna devotees moved in.

Harrison's journey into Krishna consciousness has taken him all over the world, but it is his various pilgrimages to holy sites in India that he sees as the highlight of his devotional life. In a 1974 questionnaire published in England's Melody Maker, he describes seeking Sri Krishna in His sacred homeland of Vrndavana as his all-time most thrilling experience. Retracing the footsteps of this entrancing, rain-cloud-coloured cow-herd was to George indescribably ecstatic.

By the fall of 1977, the eighty-one-year-old Srila Prabhupada's health was beginning to seriously deteriorate. George was informed of his guru's condition by his old friend Syamasundar during one of Harrison's semi-regular visits to Bhaktivedanta Manor.

"Will he live?" George asked. "He's in no immediate danger, but it doesn't really look too promising," replied the devotee sadly.

That afternoon, George revved up the engine of his jet-black Ferrari and took a long, fast drive through Oxfordshire's winding back roads - something he often did when he needed to get away from the unrelenting swoosh of his lifestyle. Meanwhile, a world away in India, a small band of Prabhupada's key men were silently chanting to themselves outside their guru's private quarters in ISKCON's Krishna-Balaram Temple in Vrndavana.

In his bed, surrounded by several solemn devotees, Prabhupada very slowly inched a simple gold ring from his finger and pressed it into the hand of one of them. "Please, give this to George Harrison. He was a good friend to us all. He loves Krishna sincerely and I love him. He was my archangel!"

Srila Prabhupada passed away on the evening of November 14, 1977.

The road to hell, they say, is straight and broad. The road to heaven, however, is narrow, rough and treacherous. One is easy; the other difficult. George Harrison's arduous spiritual trek was fraught with disappointment and pain almost from the beginning. In 1967, after finally coming to grips with the tug of his inner voice, he began a frantic search for someone or something that could help him on his way. "I used to laugh when I read about Cliff Richard being a Christian," Harrison has said "I still cringe when I hear about it, but I know now that religion and God are the only things that exist. I know some people think I'm a nut case. I find it hard not to myself, sometimes, because I still see so many things in an ordinary way. But I know that when you believe, it's real and nice. Not believing, it's all confusion and emptiness."

CHAPTER SIX

GOD'S EYE

After thirty-one years n n the job, Harry Harrison was only too happy to permanently park his bus when, in 1965, George generously offered his dad an early retirement. "So how much are you making these days?" asked the junior Harrison during one of his now infrequent trips north on a weekend sabbatical from the band.

"Around ten quid", Harry replied.

"A day?" asked George incredulously.

When his father told him no, that was what he was taking home weekly, George was adamant. "I'll give you five times that for sitting around doing nothing."

"Son," Harry shot back, smiling broadly, "you've got yourself a deal!"

The next order of business for the Harrisons' upwardly mobile young son was to purchase for his parents a modern new home in the village of Appleton, a smart suburb near Warrington, in Cheshire.

"It was lovely," said Harry. "Very private on three splendid acres of gardens. I think George paid around £10,000, but it was worth every penny. Upstairs, there was a lovely, long room we used for entertaining. Pattie and Louise talked together quite a bit about the furniture as I recall. Eventually they settled on a modern look. I was lost to all that myself though, and mainly looked after the outdoor work with the gardener."

For the Harrisons their new home was a treat. Unfortunately, they spent only five happy years there together before Louise became seriously ill and died, on July 7, 1970. For everyone in George's family, it was a crushing blow.

Once Mrs. Harrison's passing was announced to the press, the genuine and immediate outpouring of love and affection for her from fans

Opposite: **Harrison meets the press, 1974**

worldwide was overwhelming. Bouquets and cards of sympathy were sent by the hundreds, both to the Harrisons' home and to Apple. A group of concerned American fans soon established the Louise F. Harrison Memorial Cancer Fund, as well as the Apple staff, all sent flowers but did not attend the private family funeral in Liverpool.

George was at his mother's bedside when she passed away. Naturally he was deeply troubled and upset by her death, but this was his Krishna conscious period and the teachings of Srila Prabhupada were of great comfort.

Despite the tragedy, by late November of that year, George's marathon three-record set, *All Things Must Pass*, was released in the States and immediately began a steady climb to number one. It remained on the charts for an incredible thirty-eight weeks. The

At the Isle of Wight festival to see Bob Dylan perform, 1969

album, with its haunting melodies and sweeping, majestic production, was the culmination of months of painstakingly hard work by Harrison and producer Phil Spector. Having been continually shortchanged as a Beatle, George Harrison had finally come into his own. Not only was the album a gripping musical masterpiece but it was also imbued with an important spiritual message. Inspired by Harrison's homespun philosophy, young people everywhere began looking inside themselves for their own answers. The album spawned two popular singles, *What Is Life* and the international megahit, *My Sweet Lord*. Almost overnight, Hare Krishna became a household word, and George Harrison was elevated, as a solo artist, to superstar status.

His next public venture, the humanitarian Concert for Bangla

With gregarious Apple / ABKCO promo man Pete Bennet, 1970

Desh, showed the world that George Harrison was more than willing to go out on a limb for a cause in which he truly believed. It was the first example of the staggering philanthropic power of rock and roll. The historic concert was the benevolent precursor of events like Live Aid, the Prince's Trust annual shows and the Amnesty International tours. George Harrison and his three famous cohorts had already shown us that rock music had a mind; now he would prove to everyone that it had a heart as well.

The cause, a bloody vendetta of terror between West Pakistan and Bangladesh, came to the attention of George through his great friend Ravi Shankar. "When I talked with him," said Shankar in an interview conducted two days following the August 1971 concerts, "he was impressed by my sincerity, and I gave him lots to read and explained the situation."

The roster of musicians slated to appear at the benefit read like a who's who of rock and roll. On drums were Ringo Starr and super sessionman Jim Keltner. Country rocker Leon Russell and Billy Preston took over on keyboards, while Eric Clapton, George Harrison and Jesse Ed Davis looked after most of the guitar work. In addition, the well-known Apple band, Badfinger, provided vocal harmonies and

Harri's on tour, 1974

With second wife, former
receptionist, Olivia, at his side,
1976

Wailing away at the now legendary
Concert for Bangladesh

strummed along on acoustic guitars. Klaus Voormann played bass, and Jim Horn, as his name implies, led the electrifying horn section. On the Indian side of things, Ravi Shankar was on hand with his sitar, accompanied by his ever-present tabla man, the portly Alla Rakha. Phil Spector was in charge of recording the historic event, and Apple man Pete Bennett with promoting it. One notable name, however, was still missing. The big question on everybody's mind was, "What about Bob Dylan?"

Ever since word about the shows first spread, there was much speculation that the ultra-reclusive Dylan might turn up to trade licks with his old pal George. Behind the scenes, Harrison was doing everything he could to make that rumour a reality. At first Bob was skeptical, but willing to listen to what Harrison had to say. "I'll consider it, man," he told George.

Dylan seemed to be tempted by Harrison's constant encouragement to leave the self-imposed isolation in which he had been living for the past five years. As the day drew near, he showed up more than once at

Opposite: **In Los Angeles, 1974**

Harrison's New York hotel to party. When the subject of the show would come up, however, the great tunesmith turned characteristically quiet. He eventually agreed to join Harrison for the final reheasal and sound check at the Garden, and depending on how things went, would let him know if he "felt like" performing.

Huddled together on the gigantic cable-strewn stage, the two men looked surprisingly inconsequential for the rock legends that they were. Strumming first through the Harrison-Dylan composition *If Not for You*, they conferred on chord changes, assisted the technical staff with their sound checks and meandered through a long list of numbers under consideration for the show.

Harrison's next solo release, the philosophical Living in the Material World of 1973, was his last major attempt to promote his Krishna beliefs en masse. Although many reviewers saw the album as somewhat self-involved and even maudlin, Harrison remained confident that those who truly needed to would hear his God-centred message. Everybody else, as usual, would either ignore the work or, worse, see it simply as an old Beatle's newest trick.

As usual with any Harrison-directed work, the album contained the talents of a mighty array of session players including Ringo Starr, Nicky Hopkins, Gary Wright and Klaus Voormann, to name but a few.

Partying with the blissed out Radha Krishna Temple, London, 1969

Inside the tastefully designed gatefold cover was a photograph of George hosting his own version of the Last Supper on the grounds of a lavish estate, dressed as a Catholic priest complete with a pair of very deadly looking six-shooters strapped to his waist. Nothing to get excited about, however - just George lampooning the established Western religious order with a parody of the materialism so prevalent in today's Christendom. The enclosed lyric sheet was illustrated with a fiery full-colour painting of Krishna as the charioteer for his friend and disciple Arjuna on the battlefield of Kurukshetra, the original setting for the celestial Bhagavadgita, Harrison's bible. Lyrically, the songs reflected the sombre musical meanderings of a very straight Hare Krishna, which Harrison still was, in spirit if not in practice. Titles like *The Lord Loves the One Who Loves the Lord*, *The Light That Has Lighted the World*, *Be Here Now* and *Don't Let Me Wait Too Long*, made it clear to everyone where the spiritually inclined ex-Beatle's head was at. Still for all its blatantly yogic overtones, the million-selling LP managed to produce one hit single in the mantra-like *Give Me Love (Give Me Peace on Earth)*, which topped the charts in America for three months.

Out of the gate like a bullet with *All Things Must Pass*, Harrison's *Living in the Material World* and the subsequent *Dark Horse* failed to

Touching down at Heathrow

catch fire with the majority of the record-buying public. While Harrison maintained that the negative reaction to the tour didn't bother him, he was, in fact, badly bruised by it. Discouraged, as well, over *Dark Horse*'s poor sales and still quietly brooding over Pattie's embarrassing departure to live with Eric Clapton, George soon sank into a deep, seemingly irreversible depression. He would not see friends, rarely went out and became verbally abusive to those around him. He also all but abandoned his spiritual practice, although there was still the heavy Krishna conscious rap. Always the rap.

Things really got bad in early 1976, when his health started to decline, partly because of his increased drinking. One day, looking into that same magnificent peer-glass in which old Sir Frank used to primp prior to seeing his clients, Harrison noticed that his eyes had turned a deep, sickly yellow. He was also rapidly losing wieght, looking more and more like one of the refugees he had worked so hard to save just five years earlier. Thumbing through Paramahansa Yogananda's Scientific Healing Affirmations,

Harrison after being stricken with a life threatening bout of hepatitis in the mid seventies

he even began chanting translated Kriya Yoga mantras aimed at restoring lost health. Eventually, though, he gave in to his new girlfriend, Olivia's, insistence that he consult a physician, and was diagnosed as having serum hepatitis. He had suffered some liver damage, for which he was prescribed large doses of vitamins. Unfortunately, Harrison didn't respond to treatment. The only positive outcome of this nightmare was that at least now he was scared, scared enough to make an effort to truly become well.

Toward that end, Olivia contacted the well-known acupuncturist to the stars, Dr. Zion Yu in California. She had first heard of the doctor after her younger brother Peter sought treatment with him following a near fatal motorcycle accident. After several visits to Dr. Yu, Harrison's condition began to steadily improve, and within a few months he seemed to be completely cured.

Following the disastrous *Dark Horse*, George recorded another marginally successful album with the rather inscrutable title of *Extra Texture - Read All About It*. Released in Britain on September 22, 1975, the LP contained several very listenable but rather depressing cuts, among them *Grey Cloudy Lies*, *This Guitar Can't Keep From Crying*, *World of Stone* and *Tired of Midnight Blue*.

Harrison's next album, the infinitely more accessible *Thirty-Three & 1/3*, seemed to indicate that he was now squarely back on musical track. Behind the scenes, however, things were still fairly tangled up. Harrison had missed his July 26, 1976, deadline by two months and when he finally arrived in L.A. to deliver the master tapes to A&M, he discovered that Jerry Moss was preparing to sue him for the delay - to the tune of a staggering $10 million.

George's response was to ring the brass at Warner Brothers and offer the album to them on the condition that they immediately buy

Opposite: At a press conference in Hollywood, 1967. Embittered by a troublesome divorce and harrassed by a series of law suits, George started off the event by singing a caustic chorus of Dylan's *Tangled Up In Blue*

out his contract with A&M. Warner agreed and made plans to prompt-ly release the LP. In appreciation, Harrison consented (for the first time in several records) to actively promote the album by travelling with Olivia to several major American cities, meeting freely with the media at each stop.

"Some of the songs," Harrison commented, "are closer to the songs and spirit of *All Things Must Pass*. This new one has a more focused production, though, and it's very positive, very up, and most of the songs are love songs and happy songs. It doesn't compare at all to the last album, *Extra Texture*. That one caught me in a less than happy mood."

It was a good thing Harrison was becoming so open to the humour

Opposite: **Dapper George, 1967**

Below: **Pausing for a nosh at Abbey Road during sessions for the Beatles' *White Album***

behind the hassles of the material world, as he was then up to his ears in litigation brought against him by the proprietors of Bright Tunes Music Corporation, who were alleging that George had lifted the tune for his *My Sweet Lord* from the Chiffons' *He's So Fine*, the 1963 classic to which they owned the rights.

The controversial case went to court in January 1976 and garnered international headlines with each and every bump and grind of the slowly moving wheels of justice. Represented by an army of high-powered copyright lawyers, Harrison sat quietly in the crowded New York City court as a barrage of nasty accusations and innuendos flew back and forth.

Though Harrison may not have been aware of the distinct similarities between the two hit tunes, somewhere along the way either he or Billy Preston inserted the critical three notes that later convinced District Judge Owen that George had indeed committed an act of plagiarism against Bright Tunes. In his final statement before the court, Owen pronounced his judgement: "Did Harrison deliberately use the music of *He's So Fine?* I do not believe he did so deliberately. Nevertheless, it is clear that *My Sweet Lord* is the very same song as *He's So Fine* with different words, and Harrison had access to *He's So Fine*. This is, under the law, infringement of copyright, and is no less so even though subconsciously accomplished."

Harrison's former manager, Allen Klein, had in 1978 - after the trial - purchased the rights to *He's So Fine* and was therefore the direct beneficiary of George's grief. The court took note of this, considering it interference by Klein, and limited the damages to what he had paid for the song - $587,000, which Harrison paid as ordered in 1981.

While promoting *Thirty-Three & 1/3*, Harrison reflected:

"I'd be willing every time I write a song if somebody will have a computer and I can just go up to the thing and sing my new song into it and the computer will say sorry or yes, ok. I'm willing to do that, because the last thing I want to do is keep spending the rest of my life

Right: **Beatle buddy, artist 'Legs'' Larry Smith, tinkles the ivories in Harrison's antique strewn front parlor**

Below: **George boating *underneath* his fairyland estate**

In Friar Park's great hall, 1983

in court, or being faced with that problem. Once you get people thinking, "Oh, well, they beat Harrison on *My Sweet Lord*, let's sue"... they can sue the world! It made me so paranoid about writing. And I thought, "God, I don't even want to touch the guitar or the piano, in case I'm touching somebody's note." Somebody might own that note, so you'd better watch out!"

Probably the only good thing to come out of the Bright Tunes ordeal for Harrison was that it gave him the inspiration to compose "This Song," a biting satire of the whole sordid affair, and the biggest tune on *Thirty-Three & 1/3.* "All in all," said a Warner Brothers official as *This Song* started its steady climb up the American charts, "Harrison picked a mighty tough way to get a hit record."

CHAPTER SEVEN

THE QUIET ONE

After his wife, Louise, died, Harry Harrison often went to visit his sons at Friar Park. Growing his striking silver hair well past his shoulders, the sixty-five-year-old began spending a lot of time with George and his friends, even joining his son on the road for the 1974 Dark Horse tour.

The elder Harrison was happier and more fulfilled than he had ever dreamed possible. Although he missed Louise terribly, he had made a good life for himself at Appleton and seemed quite content to putter about in the garden, or take a stroll down to his local pub for a friendly pint or two with his mates.

One evening in May 1978, George and Olivia went to bed early after a particularly exhausting day. Sometime during the night George became aware of a dull blue and gold light ringing the darkened room. Suddenly, there was his father, standing solemnly in the middle of the large room looking lovingly down at his astonished son. After a moment or two, Harry quietly bade George and his brothers farewell and then disappeared. That same day, at his home in Cheshire, Harry Harrison died of emphysema, related to a lifetime of very heavy smoking. Although everyone was saddened and upset, George was comforted somewhat by what he considered to be his father's spiritually auspicious passing.

On August 1, 1978, George and Olivia's only child, Dhani, was born at the Princess Christian Nursing Home in Windsor, just a short hop down the highway from Friar Park. Dhani is the Sanskrit word for "wealthy," but Harrison insists he was only aware of its significance as a term relating to his beloved Indian music. So excited was George by the birth of his son and heir that he rushed down to his friend Rodney

Opposite: **In Australia with a new friend**

Turner's in Henley to pick up a new baby-blue Rolls-Royce he had ordered in celebration of the great event. Harrison was like a man reborn. So concerned and possessive was he that, for the next few months, only he and Olivia were allowed to touch young Dhani. Like John Lennon after his son Sean was born, George was frantic that the baby might "pick up" something if handled by anyone. These Beatles, it seems, take their babies very seriously.

George and Olivia invited her parents to fly over from California to be the sole guests at their secret wedding on September 2 at the Henley Registry Office. Sometime later, the happy couple treated themselves to a luxurious honeymoon in Tunisia. By the time they returned, George was anxious to get back to work.

Harrison's first musical project following his father's passing and Dhani's arrival was the masterfully conceived and lyrically brilliant George Harrison, issued in England on February 23, 1979. The LP featured ten thoughtful new tracks and was once again infused with Harrison's familiar Krishna-conscious philosophy, only this time presented in a far more palatable manner, sandwiched as it was between a lot of genuinely great music. "It's the first time I've done a birth, a marriage and a death during making a record," says George. "We had a lot of stoppages, but I don't think it really took any longer than any other album to record. The other night Mick Ralphs from Bad Company said to me, 'Do you feel like you're in the after-the-album lull?' And I said, 'I'm in that while I'm making it.'"

By 1980, George was beginning to feel that the time was right to record another album. Gathering together an array of old friends - Ringo, Alla Rakha, Ray Cooper, Herbie Flowers, Willie Weeks, Al Kooper, Jim Keltner and Tom Scott - Harrison began sessions at Friar Park for what would later become Somewhere in England. The album Harrison submitted to Warner Brothers records in Los Angeles consisted of eight new tracks as well as two old standard, "Baltimore Oriole" and "Hong Kong Blues." It also included a suitably slick, sophisticated cover photo of George's profile merged with a satellite shot of a cloudy Great Britain. Warner Brothers unfortunately was not particularly impressed with either the music or art and tersely rejected the album. In the end, four tracks were cut - "Flying Hour," "Lay His Head," "Sat Singing" and "Tears of the World" - and in their place, four new "Harrisongs" were added, "Tear Drops," "Blood From a Clone," "That Which I Have Lost" and "All Those Years Ago." A new cover was also put together by Ray Cooper and photographer Caroline Irwin. The album, released in June 1981, spawned two singles, "Tear Drops" and "All Those Years Ago," Harrison's touching tribute to his late partner, John Lennon.

George Harrison was at home sleeping when the phone rang. The jarring noise startled him, and left him shaking. Before he even touched the receiver he felt that something must be wrong. The wavering, crackling line told him instantly that the call was from overseas - it was Louise, Harrison's eldest sister, who had lived stateside for many years. George quickly began to prepare himself for what he

was sure must be bad news.

That afternoon in London, the Beatles' former promo man, Derek Taylor, wandered over to Apple's last sorry incarnation on St. James Street to sit with the company's managing director, Neil Aspinall, and wait for the calls to start flooding in. John Lennon had been shot dead by a maniac at point-blank range on December 8, 1980, as he and Yoko were returning from a late-night mixing session for a tune called *Walking on Thin Ice*. After a couple of awkward hours spent painfully reminiscing, Taylor and Aspinall said goodbye. Derek walked into the street and caught a cab to George Harrison's London office. A short time later, he summoned up the courage to finally ring George. After a decade spent on the phone, this was one call he dreaded. "George, maybe you should make some sort of statement, just to get the bastards off your back."

"I can't now," Harrison replied. There was a long pause. "Later, maybe."

The line suddenly clicked off. Taylor replaced the receiver and lit a cigarette. He didn't want to push the issue, but his better judgement told him that the longer George waited to speak, the worse it would

With the dolphins at Seaworld, Brisbane, Australia, 1982

With Eric Idle and an unidentified fan in the mid seventies

ultimately be. Less than an hour later he was back on the line to the Park. This time George agreed to help the misty-eyed PR man formulate a statement for the press:

"After all we went through together I had and still have great love and respect for him (John Lennon). I am shocked and stunned. To rob life is the ultimate robbery in life. This perpetual encroachment on other people's space is taken to the limit with the use of a gun. It is an outrage that people can take other people's lives when they obviously haven't got their own lives in order."

Recorded at Friar Park studios, *All Those Years Ago* was originally intended as a vehicle for Ringo. But following Lennon's murder in December 1980, it was rewritten by George to include specific reference to the tragedy. On the spur of the moment, Harrison decided it would be fitting if he were joined on the session by Ringo and Paul. Happily, they agreed, thus making it the first and only Beatles' reunion of the new decade. Produced with the help of George Martin, the song included backup vocals by Linda McCartney and Denny Laine, who tells me he has yet to be paid for the session! Although it was a pretty bleak circumstance under which to record a new "Beatle" song, it was nevertheless a touching gesture. The tune rose to number two on the charts and remains a popular jukebox hit in North America to this day.

The unlikely harbinger of Harrison's renewed enthusiasm for his art came in the person of affable country rocker Carl Perkins, one of George's earliest and most important musical influences. Perkins, fifty-three, was musically as sharp as ever, but in the past few years had experienced a serious slump in his remarkable career. How ironic that the musician who helped inspire Harrison to pick up the guitar in the first place would be responsible for bringing him back into the fold. Seriously considering retirement himself, Perkins and his manager cooked up the idea of a star-studded rockabilly extravaganza featuring the creme de la creme of the pop world in a concert designed to showcase Perkin's exceptional talents.

To that end, he videotaped personalised invitations to Ringo Starr, Eric Clapton, Dave Edmunds and George Harrison, among others. Within ten days, Perkins had received notes of acceptance from everyone he contacted, with the exception of George. "I thought I was wasting my time," Perkins told People magazine, "because I read that (George) would never go before a live audience again." Several days later, however, Harrison enthusiastically accepted, and the big show was on. Perkins's people engineered a lucrative deal with the Cinemax cable network in the United States to air the one-hour special, entitled "Blue Suede Shoes."

After the shocking death of John Lennon, George dedicated the song *All Those Years Ago* to his memory

Perkins wasn't the first of his peers to try to coax George onstage after his unhappy tour of America in 1974. New York promoter Sid Bernstein attempted to get the Beatles together for an internationally televised benefit in 1979 to aid Cambodia's boat people, as did United Nations secretary gental Kurt Waldheim for another concert later that year. Both efforts, unfortunately, failed to convince Harrison to perform, as did Bob Geldof, Live Aid's patron saint, in his bid for the guitarist to participate in his star-studded extravaganza. Until Carl Perkins ambled onto the scene in late 1985, most observers doubted whether Harrison would ever perform onstage again.

The evening of the taping on October 21 at Limehouse Studios in London, Harrison was a bundle of nerves. He paced anxiously around his dressing room, chain-smoking. Then, balancing on the arm of a sofa, he tuned and returned his vintage Gibson. Onstage, sensing George's butterflies, Perkins immediately eased the situation by inviting the studio audience to clap along to *Everybody's Trying to Be My Baby*. Even before the end of that first song, Harrison had regained his confidence and was relishing the spotlight after so many years spent in self-imposed exile. "George Harrison, everybody!" yelled Perkins as the audience exploded with applause. "Don't he look good?" By the time Perkins, George and Dave Edmunds ripped into the classic *Your True Love*, it was obvious to everyone that Harrison was having the time of his life.

Meanwhile, Olivia stood watching in the wings, not caring that the large tears streaming down her face were making a mess of her make-up. George was back! Not just for his old buddies and the fans, but for her and Dhani and, best of all, for himself. It was perhaps the single happiest night of their married life. "I haven't seem him so happy in years," she commented later to the press. "That's my old George!"

From that moment on, Harrison was suddenly wild about sharing his music with the world once again. When he wasn't in the studio writing or recording, he was jamming with friends at any one of a number of exotic locations. In February 1987, he and Bob Dylan went along to see guitarist Jesse Ed Davis play with the Graffiti Band at the Palomino Club in North Hollywood. Before the night was out, both of them were up onstage playing their hearts out. Overnight, it seemed, George Harrison was one of the hottest things going, and this time he was ready for action.

George's next major public appearance came four months later on June 5 and 6. The occasion was the Prince's Trust annual charity concerts at Wembley Stadium, just outside London. As usual, rumours of an impending Beatles reunion were rife, but came to nothing. When the lights went down and Eric Clapton stepped up to the mike to introduce George and Ringo, the audience was ecstatic. Even half a loaf, when it came to the Beatles, was something to shout about. Harrison and Clapton traded lead licks on a shining version of *While My Guitar Gently Weeps*, followed by a remarkably touching rendition of *Here Comes the Sun*, which also featured George's new musical colleague, Jeff Lynne, formerly of the "Beatlesque" Electic Light Orchestra.

The *Magical Mystery Tour* bus during a break in filming

Another big night for George Harrison came on January 20, 1988, when the Beatles were inducted into the Rock 'n' Roll Hall of Fame at the Waldorf Astoria Hotel in Manhattan. "They had long hair, scruffy clothes, but they had a record contract," joked presenter Mick Jagger at the official ceremony. "I was almost sick! I'm really proud to be the one who leads them into the Hall of Fame." It was a fabulous night. George, Ringo, and Julian and Sean Lennon took the stage with an unusually frumpy-looking Yoko Ono. The only damper on the splendid evening came when word leaked out that Paul McCartney would not be making the trip.

At the time of the Hall of Fame induction, Harrison's single, *Got My Mind Set on You*, was securely in the Top Ten and was rapidly heading for number one. For once, Beatle Paul was dramatically overshadowed by his introspective mate from Wavertree.

Despite the controversy over Paul's absence, George was enthusiastic when the time came for him to say a few words on behalf of the group. "I don't have much to say," he began, "because I'm the quiet Beatle. We all know why John can't be here, and I'm sure he would be, and it's really hard to stand here supposedly representing the Beatles ...what's left, I'm afraid. But we all loved him so much.... It's unfortunate that Paul's not here, because he was the one who had the speech in his pocket!"

**Opposite: Shooting the Beatles'
Magical Mystery Tour debacle**

George's next album release following the Gone Troppo fiasco took

Squire Harrison in his fancy home recording studio

Opposite: **Promoting the Beatles' popular animated feature,** *Yellow Submarine,* **1968**

place on November 2, 1987 with the issuance of Cloud Nine.

Among the talents assembled for the album were Harrison's usual stable of superstar musicians, including Ringo, Jim Keltner, Gary Wright, Ray Cooper and Eric Clapton. Two relative newcomers to Friar Park Studios were Elton John and Jeff Lynne.

Lynne and Harrison were originally brought together by well-known British rocker Dave Edmunds. For years Harrison had been an ardent admirer of Lynne's extravagant Electric Light Orchestra.

The sweeping success of Cloud Nine went a long way toward helping to re-establish Harrison as the major artist his many fans always knew he was. For the first time in several years, the name George Harrison once again translated into big ratings on radio and television. The album opened up a whole new audience of young people to the life and work of this reluctant world legend.

Harrison was also part of the magnificent Travelling Wilburys. It was the first time George had been a member of a bona fide band in eighteen years. The inception of the big-name group, consisting of Bob Dylan, Roy Orbison, Tom Petty, Jeff Lynne and George, came about rather casually as an outgrowth of the Cloud Nine project. In

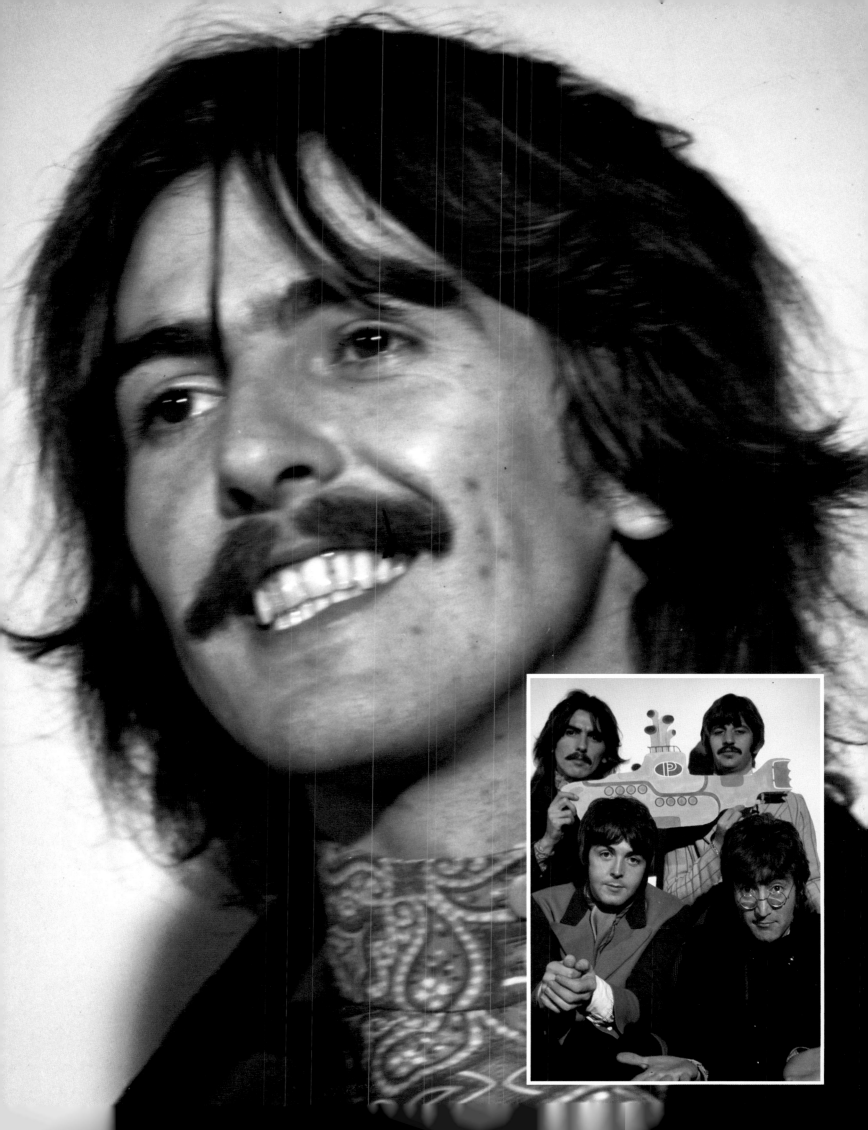

April 1988, Harrison was in Los Angeles tying up some loose ends regarding the hit album when Warner Brothers asked him to consider recording a new tune to back the twelve-inch extended-play version of the popular *This is Love.*

George, however, couldn't really think of anything he had back at Friar Park that would be suitable, and so mentioned his dilemma to Lynne and Orbison during dinner at a swanky L.A. eatery. George suggested that the three of them book some studio time and record something together. Orbison and Lynne readily agreed. Bearing in mind the time restraints placed upon the trio by the record company, Lynne suggested asking Bob Dylan if they might use his private studio, located in the garage of his luxurious Malibu home. A few days later, Harrison dropped by Tom Petty's house to pick up a guitar for the session and on the spur of the moment invited Petty to join them. George and Jeff wrote the tune together the next day in the studio and then persuaded Dylan to sit in as well.

After the five old pros layed down the musical tracks for the upbeat folksy number, they sat together in Dylan's garden on a lunch break and wrote the words. "Okay, you guys," said Harrison, smiling broadly, "We're all supposed to be such hot stuff, how about some lyrics, then?" Spying a discarded cardboard box sporting a bright orange sticker that said "Handle With Care," they had their title, and by the time it was over a major hit as well.

So pleased were they with the finished track that Harrison decided it was far too good to simply be stuck on the B side of one of his singles. He suggested they do an album together. The sessions went on for about two weeks, with some additional work done in England at Friar Park. The group's sidemen, dubbed "The Sideburys" by Harrison, included Jim Keltner, percussionist Ray Cooper, Ian Wallace playing the tom-toms and Jim Horn wailing away on sax.

Lynne and Harrison came up with the name Travelling Wilburys from a joke bandied about during the long, eight-month sessions for Cloud Nine. Apparently, someone coined the phrase "tremblin' wilburys" to describe the unwelcome little screwups and glitches that occurred while they were recording the multitrack masters, and the name stuck. A full year before he even thought of putting a group together, Harrison had some custom guitar picks made up that had "Travelling Wilburys" printed along the top.

In keeping with the zany spirit of the album, the five co-conspirators decided to adopt bizarre new Wilbury names. Harrison took the alias Nelson Wilbury, while Dylan assumed the name Lucky; Petty was Charlie T., while Orbison was called Lefty. The album, entitled *The Travelling Wilburys: Volume One*, was released on October 25, 1988, on the newly formed Wilbury Records label. Distributed by Warner Brothers, it contained ten tracks and a tongue-in-cheek history lesson on the origins of the Wilbury clan penned by one Hugh Hampton E.F. Norti-Blitz, better known as Monty Python's brilliant Michael Palin.

MTV in America premiered the classy "Handle With Care" video with much fanfare on October 25, and within a few short weeks the

Opposite: **Harrison views his beloved Formula One auto racing nonsense**

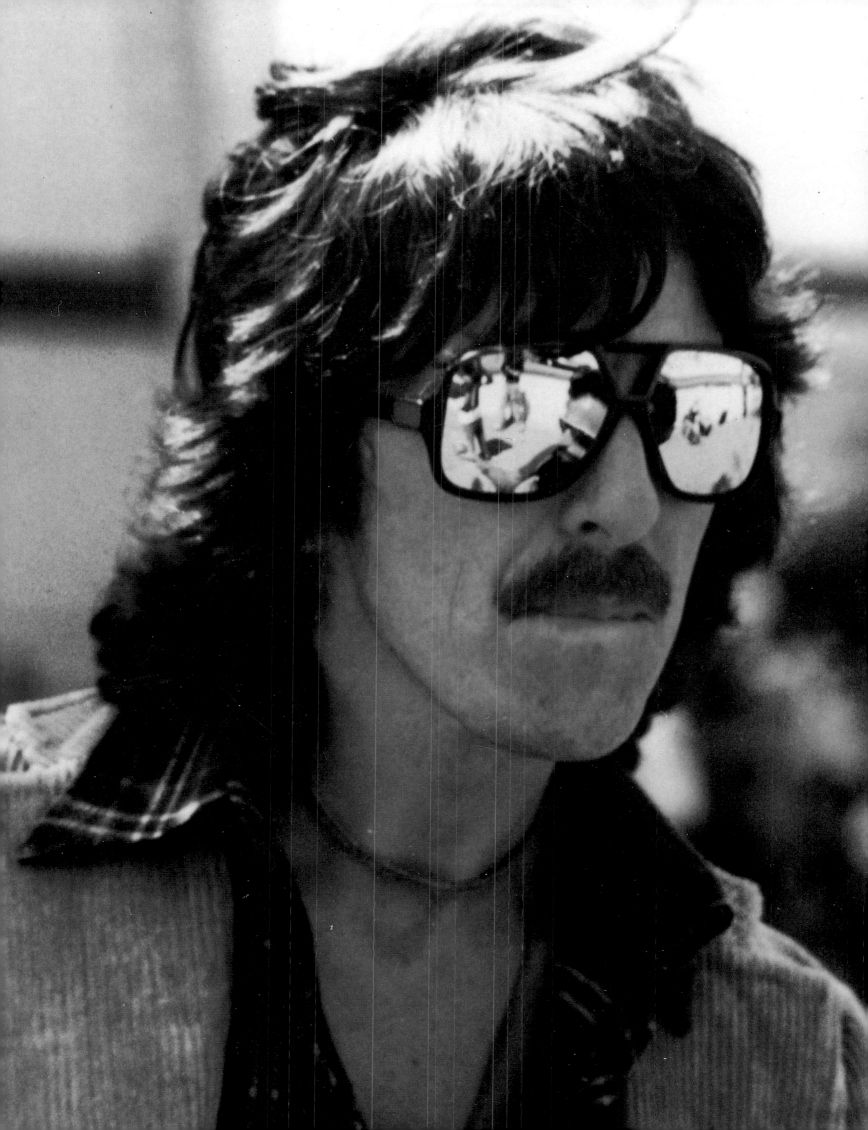

George Harrison, a man who definitely loves his cars

album was selling like hotcakes on both sides of the Atlantic. There was talk of a Wilbury tour, scheduled for sometime in the new year, while Volume Two was eagerly awaited by a whole new breed of Wilburymaniacs.

The staggering success of the band was a boon to George after so many years of brooding over the musical malaise of the record industry. But it was the energising effect on Roy Orbison's career that secretly pleased Harrison the most. In his final interview, Orbison praised Harrison for persuading him to join the Wilburys at a time when his solo career had taken a turn for the worse.

The Wilburys' curtain however came crashing to the ground with the sudden death of Orbison on December 6, 1988, from a massive heart attack. Upon hearing the tragic news, George told reporters that Roy was "a sweet, sweet man. We loved Roy, and still do. He's out there, really, his spirit. You know, life flows on within you and without you. He's around."